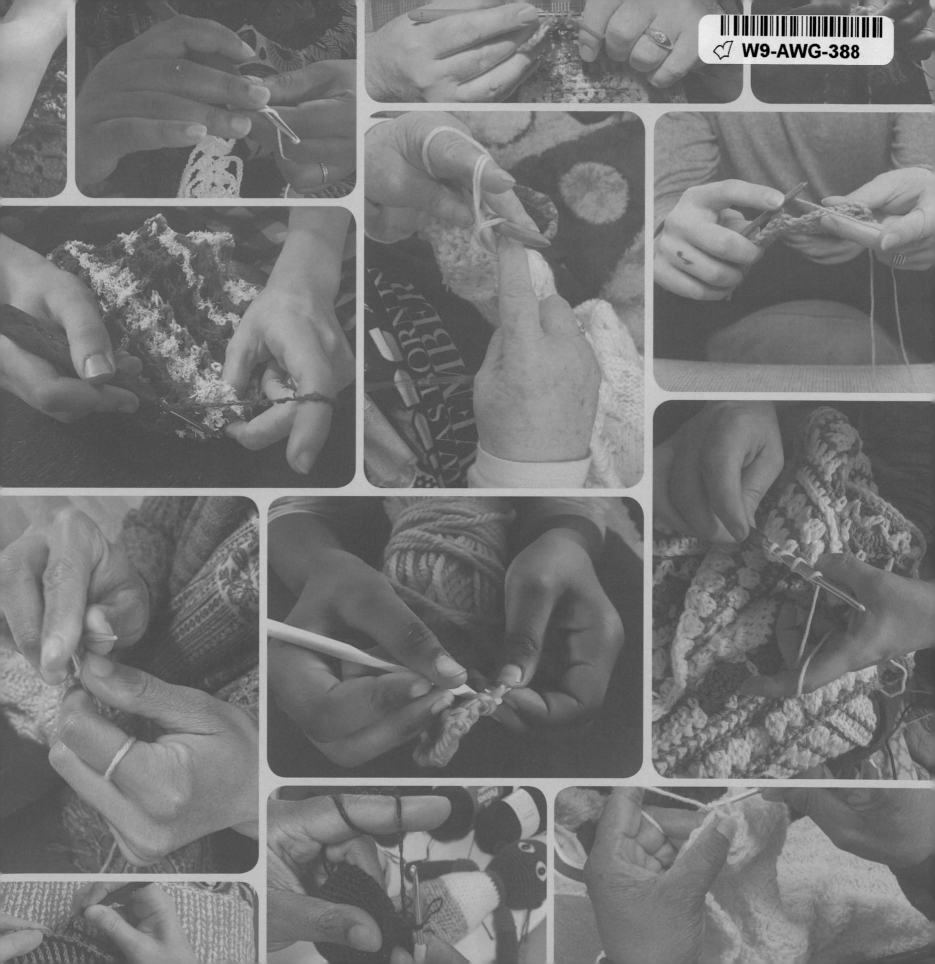

Hello, CROCHET Friends!

Making Art, Being Mindful, Giving Back: *Do What Makes You Happy*

Jonah Larson
WITH Jennifer Larson

KWiL Publishing

Photography by Erin Harris and from the Larson Family Archive

Design by Karl Engebretson

I dedicate this book to my two mothers—
the one who brought me into this world
and the one who guides me through it.

—Jonah Larson

To my father Clarence Domask, who left me far too soon
and taught me the value of hard work.

To Dr. Jeff Thompson, whose wisdom and
encouragement made me stronger.

To my son Leif, who made me believe in miracles.

To my daughter Mercy, who made our family complete.

And to my husband Christopher, who makes me laugh
and tucks me in every night.

—Jennifer Larson

Published by KWiL Publishing, Milwaukee, Wisconsin, USA. www.kwilpublishing.com

LCCN 2019937347 | ISBN 9780999143704

First edition July 2019

Printed in the United States of America by Worzalla in Stevens Point, Wisconsin

Book design by Karl Engebretson.
Typography in this book plays with the typefaces Henderson Slab & Henderson Sans, designed by Alejandro Paul, from Sudtipos,
as well as the typefaces Le Monde Courrier and Le Monde Sans, designed by Jean François Porchez, from Typofonderie.

Hello, **CROCHET** Friends!

Making Art, Being Mindful, Giving Back: *Do What Makes You Happy*

Hello, crochet friends! It's me, Jonah.
Thank you so much for reading my book.
I really hope that you enjoy it.

I love crochet because it is a way to make art,
be mindful, and give back. Crochet makes me
happy. I hope that by reading this book, you will
be inspired to find something (maybe crochet?)
in your life that makes *you* happy.

ETHIOPIA

Ethiopian Highlands

Like most stories,
mine starts at
the beginning —
the very beginning
of my life.

I don't remember ETHIOPIA.
I can't see my birth mother's face.
I have no memory of the orphanage
that took me in as a baby.

But I do know my story.
My parents have told it to me
for as long as I can remember.

A village in Ethiopia

IT GOES LIKE THIS:

My birth mother left me wrapped in a banana leaf
under a tree, protected from the sun, near a water
trail where she knew I would be found.

As she did every morning, a local woman named
Zenebech set out from her home to get water
for the day.

Only on that morning, after hearing the cries of a
baby, she came home with water AND... ... ...

ME!

"This is me sleeping in a crib at the orphanage."

Zenebech wanted to keep me, but she already had children of her own. She took me to an orphanage in the small town of Durame.

"This is Zenebech, the woman who found me."

I was given the name Faiso, which she said meant saved under the sun. It is still my middle name.

I think it must have been hard for my birth mother to leave me, but she must have thought I would have a better life.

"Here I am meeting my big brother Leif for the very first time."

"Here I am with my mom and dad, on a plane, heading for Wisconsin!"

After working very hard to save enough money and waiting for a long time, my mom and dad saw me for the first time on July 4, 2008, a good date for a new American!

I was very sick, and the orphanage almost didn't let me go. Eventually they did, but it was a very hard trip for me and my parents. Fortunately, I don't remember, but they sure do.

JONAH:
Hey, Mom. What was Ethiopia like?

JENNIFER:
Jonah, I remember how loving the community was. Everyone wanted the best for all of the children.

One of the hardest things for me during this time was feeling like I was taking you, a child, away from his culture.

I worried, very much, that I was taking you away from what you were supposed to be.

While we were there, we got to know everyone in the community so well. They trusted us with their Ethiopian baby, but they also told us,

"Don't let him forget where he came from."

At home in La Crosse, Wisconsin, my health got better quickly.

I was a happy baby, and as soon as I could, I followed my big brother LEIF around everywhere!

Here are Leif and I meeting Mercy for the very first time!

Within a year, my parents were on their way back to Ethiopia. They came home with my new baby sister, Mihret. Her name means mercy, so that is what we call her, MERCY.

She came from the same orphanage that had taken care of me. We both come from the Kambaata people.

Here I am with Mercy wearing traditional clothing that my mom brought home from Ethiopia.

By the time I was three, I was walking, talking, AND... ... ...

...READING!

My parents took me to a special reading program. I was a quick learner and reading and doing advanced math very early.

I wasn't quite so good at being a "friend," which is what my daycare called the children. I'm not very proud of it now, but I got kicked out of not one, not two, but *three* daycare centers.

At one I refused to take a nap or participate in quiet time. I would walk around and take the blankets off the other "friends" so they couldn't sleep. Apparently, other kids' parents were complaining to the daycare because their children were falling asleep on their dinner plates!

As I got older, school and classroom work were kind of boring for me, and I really didn't like to follow the rules. I would finish my work quickly and then think of other ways to entertain myself. My brain was always working, although what I found entertained *me* often became someone else's distraction.

One year, after getting *57* behavior slips, my parents suggested that the teacher stop sending them home because they thought I was collecting them.
(I was!)

That same year in art one day, I poured paint on the floor and slid across the room on my belly. That didn't go over well with my teacher, or the principal, or the custodian. I like to think of those days as my *"rascal"* years, but I know now that it was more than just a little mischief.

I made my teacher cry, I tore up my classmates' work, and I threw my shoes. My parents often had to leave work to pick me up, and sometimes my mom would have to stay home with me when I made *really* bad choices.

I DIDN'T WANT TO ACT UP, BUT I DID.

JONAH:

Hey, Mom. Do you remember what you were thinking during those years?

JENNIFER:

I always knew that you were inherently a good child. You were clearly so smart and charming and gifted. What I didn't know was how you were going to use those gifts. There were two paths, and I so badly wanted you to follow the successful one. We poured our whole lives into it.

Pouring paint on the floor!?

That doesn't sound like our Jonah!

Six years later, we still have (and use!) my very first dishcloth. And this is the hook that started it all!

My aunt dropped off a bag of leftover craft items that she thought we could use for art projects. I quickly searched the bag for potential treasure. A shiny, thin metal tool of some sort caught my eye. "What is this?" I asked my mom. "What do you do with it?"

My mom grabbed her tablet and typed "beginner crochet" in the search box. She pressed *return*, and the screen filled with "How To" videos for scarves, hats, mittens and… an octopus! Sweet! I had found my first project!

Bringing me back to my five-year-old reality, my mom suggested that I should start with something easier, like a… dishcloth. I knew I'd come back to that octopus someday, but for now I grabbed my shiny new crochet hook, pressed *play*, and my world changed.

Can you believe it?
Tearing up work, making people cry?

Don't worry. Things get better.
Much better. But first, we have to go back to one day when I was five.

At first I didn't know anything about crochet. I didn't know that crochet hooks came in different sizes. (I only had one!) I didn't know there were patterns. I didn't know what a skein was (it's the crochet term for a ball of yarn), and I surely didn't know how to pronounce that word! (It's "skane.")

Maybe most importantly, I didn't know that some people believed the stereotype that boys don't crochet. I didn't care. I liked that crocheting made me happy.

Before long I was making more elaborate items like cowls and mermaid blankets and, of course, that octopus.

One summer I took some of my pieces to our local county fair. My mom secretly entered a few of my items in the "open" class, and I won several blue ribbons. That was nice, but really, I just liked making beautiful things.

Over the years, I have made hats, mittens, scarves, baskets, blankets, doilies, ornaments, stuffed animals, pillows, dishcloths, bags, and even baby booties! If you name it, I've probably made it!

Even though I was getting good at crochet, school was still rough. I was continuing to get in trouble. I knew my parents were getting worried about me, and I think I was in danger of getting kicked out of school.

My parents met with the teachers, the principal, and the school counselors. They all wanted to help me be successful, but nothing seemed to be working.

Nothing, until a teacher asked me if I wanted to bring my crochet to school. My older brother worried (he's very protective of me) that I might get picked on, but I wanted to give it a try.

WHY? Because at home, I had begun to notice something that I hadn't expected and at first did not understand.

When I was crocheting, I didn't feel jumpy or jittery. I didn't feel like I needed to do something to get attention. My mind was quiet, calm, and peaceful. I was happy to sit by my mom and focus on my project. I wondered, "Could the same thing happen at school?"

Here I am with Mrs. Quick, my fifth grade teacher who changed my life by inviting me to crochet in her classroom.

The first day I brought in my crochet project, I put the yarn and hook in my desk. As usual, I finished my work early and felt the "rascal" thoughts begin. This time, instead of throwing my shoe across the room or tearing up my classmate's work, I reached into my desk, grabbed my hook and yarn, and started to… you guessed it… crochet away!

My classmates didn't make fun of me. They thought it was great, and they were surprised by how fast my fingers moved. Some of them even wanted to try crocheting. (I think that they were secretly just very happy that I wasn't tearing up their artwork!)

Throughout the fifth grade, whenever I felt some kind of bad behavior starting up, I would take out my project and crochet away the urge to do something disruptive. Since then, my parents have not once had to pick me up from school early.

(Except for the day I caught my hand in the bleachers and my dad had to take me in for stitches. Don't worry! I was still able to crochet!)

JONAH:
Mom, what were you thinking during this time?

JENNIFER:
Jonah, it was magical.

Finding crochet was, I believe, therapeutic for you. Through it you grew mindful not just of your stitches, but more mindful of your life. While you were crocheting, you had time to think about — to process — your choices, and there was a direct connection between having this time and making better choices.

The calmness that you experienced while you were crocheting seemed to extend into your life as a whole. You found an outlet through crochet. I hope that other kids can find their outlets, too.

17

I help a group of crocheters make soap sacks. S.A.C.K. stands for "Supporting a Community with Kindness." The sacks are crocheted cotton bags that hold a bar of soap and double as a washcloth. We give them to people in need.

Finally, things were better at school, and at home I was usually crocheting close to five hours a day!

Like so many other crocheters, I love donating or gifting my items best, and sometimes my work is auctioned to raise money. For example, once I made a big, beautiful afghan (a blanket) in warm golden colors with loop yarn using only my fingers. At an auction raising money for an animal rescue organization, it sold for $200! My dog Bella was rescued, so I especially loved this.

I also make sure that I give back to my birth country. My favorite place to give to is Roots Ethiopia, an organization doing charitable work in the region where Mercy and I were born.

When it was clear that my crocheting was here to stay, my mom joined some online crochet communities and started an Instagram page.

I had a small group of people who followed me and liked my work. I also started my own business, Jonah's Hands. I have learned a lot about running a business. I had to get my own bank account, learn how to price my items, and how to purchase supplies. (I like to look for sales and clip coupons!)

I do four things with my money. I save some, I donate some, I invest some, and I spend some. Every now and then I take the whole family out to dinner, and I pick up the check. After all, my whole family plays an important role. My sister is the yarn winder, my brother helps me with my YouTube channel, my dad drives me to the yarn stores and models my hats, and my mom… well, there wouldn't be a Jonah's Hands without her.

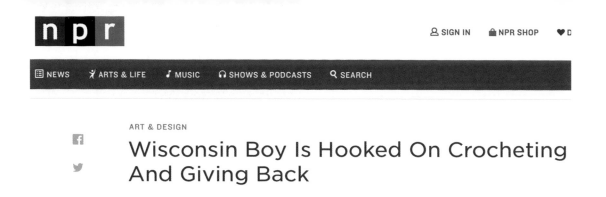
ART & DESIGN

Wisconsin Boy Is Hooked On Crocheting And Giving Back

Jonah Larson, La Crosse crochet prodigy, sets up a GoFundMe to help Ethiopian village where he was born

Amy Schwabe, **Milwaukee Journal Sentinel**   Published 11:12 a.m. CT Feb. 25, 2019

≡
MENU   **Tribune** LA CROSSE   News   Obituaries   Sports   Our 7 Rivers   Buy & Sell   ☁ 67°   👤   🔍

La Crosse boy a globally renowned crochet prodigy at age 11

Emily Pyrek La Crosse Tribune   Jan 15, 2019   💬 4

One day I was in my usual spot on the sofa sitting across from my mom and making a cowl when we got a call from our local newspaper. They were interested in doing a story about me. I wasn't sure why I deserved a story, but I thought it would be fun.

Almost immediately after that story was published, I had requests for interviews from other newspapers, radio stations, and even television shows! My following on social media grew (a lot!), and I got so many orders (thousands!) I had to temporarily close shop to catch up. I can crochet fast, but not that fast!

So many kind people have sent me yarn!

Everything that has happened since then has been *amazing*. I have been able to expand my business, partner with organizations to raise even more money for charity, and connect with incredibly kind and generous people from all over the world.

All of this because of my very favorite thing—all of this because of CROCHET.

21

WHAT IS CROCHET?

Crochet is working with a

HOOK
+ **YARN** to make
STITCHES

You combine stitches by following (or making up) a pattern, which provides the directions for...

(BOOM!)

...completing a project.

"I think crochet brings beauty and joy to people all over the world."

THE HOOK IS YOUR TOOL.

I mostly use the pencil hold.

The knife hold.

You use a crochet hook to pull one loop of yarn through another loop of yarn.

Hooks are usually held in one of two ways, and they come in different sizes and materials including wood, plastic, and metal.

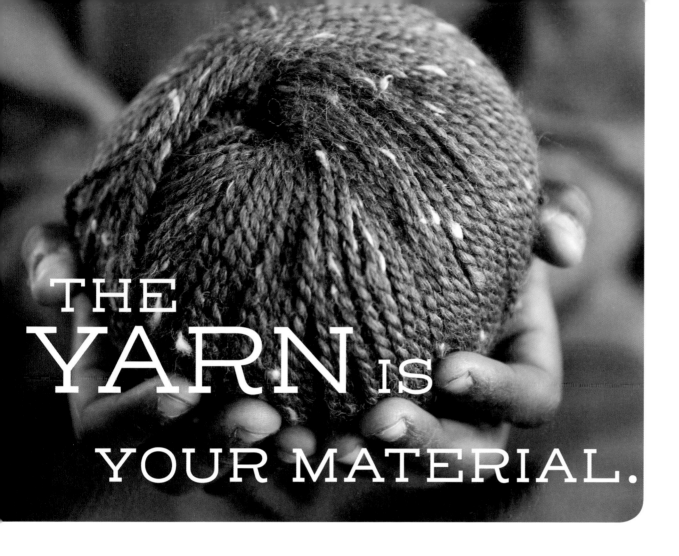

THE YARN IS YOUR MATERIAL.

Wool

"I like to test myself to see if I can identify the fibers in a yarn without looking at the label. Do they come from animals (wool) or plants (cotton)? Are they synthetic (not made from animals or plants)? Or a blend?

Cotton

You pick your yarn's fiber, color, and weight depending on your project or pattern. (Or, if you are like me, you pick your project depending on your yarn!)

"Shades of orange just glow and warm my heart. Whenever I look at them, my mood brightens. I feel happy. When I make things using gray and blue, I feel a little... gray and blue myself!"

I usually guess correctly, but once in a while I get tricked. One time, I felt some super soft yarn that I thought had come from a sheep, but it actually had come from a musk ox! I have no idea how you would get wool from musk oxen. They don't look very approachable or cooperative!

Synthetic

THE STITCHES

ARE YOUR WORK.

You loop your yarn in specific ways to make different stitches.

Single, double, and treble crochet are the three foundational stitches. Once you have learned these, there are hundreds and hundreds more you can try, and you can even make up your own!

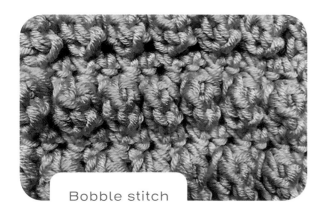

Bobble stitch

Waffle stitch

Moss stitch

"If I'm using my favorite hook and a smooth yarn, my fingers will suddenly take off in a burst of speed like a little Usain Bolt sprinting in a 100-stitch crochet race."

And remember…

HOOK
+ **YARN** to make
STITCHES =

(BOOM!)

Another beautiful project complete!

CROCHET

"I am so thankful for the people I have met and the heartwarming
FRIENDS
messages and beautiful gifts I have received."

Michael Sellick (aka Mikey)

FOUNDER OF THE CROCHET CROWD

CANADA

Jose Ideildo da Silva Junior

@JUNIORCROCHETEIRO

BRAZIL

Frana Biederman

OWNER OF PHI BETA PACA™: ALPACAS & YARNS

NEW MEXICO, UNITED STATES

Fasika Abay Monfraix

@ETHIO_CROCHET

FRANCE

Michelle Buckhanan

OWNER OF YARN JUNKIE & GIFTS

WISCONSIN, UNITED STATES

Grace Bower

"GRAMMY GRACE"

NEW ZEALAND/ AOTEAROA

Justine Correira

ALASKA, UNITED STATES

Elaine Ashby

HENRYETTA'S HOOKS & NEEDLES

UNITED KINGDOM

"Mikey, Jose, Frana, Fasika, Michelle, Grace, Justine, and Elaine are some of the many crochet friends I have connected with from so many countries around the... ... ...

*"From La Crosse, Wisconsin, USA,
I have connected with crochet friends
in 136 countries and counting."* •

CANADA

UNITED STATES

THE BAHAMAS

MEXICO

CUBA

HAITI DOMINICAN REPUBLIC

GUATEMALA BELIZE JAMAICA ANTIGUA & BARBUDA
HONDURAS SAINT LUCIA
EL SALVADOR BARBADOS

NICARAGUA GRENADA

...WORLD.

COSTA RICA TRINIDAD
PANAMA & TOBAGO
VENEZUELA
COLUMBIA

ECUADOR

PERU

FIJI

BOLIVIA

PARAGUAY

CHILE

URUGUAY

NEW ZEALAND

"It's almost as though all of our crochet hooks

ICELAND
NORWAY
SWEDEN
FINLAND
ESTONIA
UNITED KINGDOM
DENMARK LATVIA
LITHUANIA
IRELAND POLAND
NETHERLANDS GERMANY
BELARUS
RUSSIA
BELGIUM AUSTRIA
LUXEMBOURG UKRAINE KAZAKHSTAN
SWITZERLAND CZECH REP. SLOVAKIA
FRANCE HUNGARY MOLDOVA MONGOLIA
CROATIA
SLOVENIA ROMANIA
MONACO ALBANIA BULGARIA UZBEKISTAN KYRGYZSTAN
MONTENEGRO MACEDONIA ARMENIA
PORTUGAL ITALY CYPRUS
SPAIN GREECE TURKEY SOUTH JAPAN
KOREA
MALTA SYRIA
MOROCCO LEBANON IRAQ AFGHANISTAN
TUNISIA ISRAEL IRAN NEPAL
ALGERIA JORDAN
LIBYA KUWAIT PAKISTAN
EGYPT
QATAR
MALI U.A.E. BANGLADESH
SAUDI ARABIA
NIGER SUDAN OMAN INDIA MYANMAR VIETNAM
ERITREA THAILAND
SENEGAL CAMBODIA
PHILIPPINES
SIERRA LEONE ETHIOPIA
SRI LANKA MALAYSIA
LIBERIA NIGERIA
SOMALIA
EQUATORIAL GUINEA SINGAPORE
UGANDA KENYA
RWANDA INDONESIA
CONGO BRAZIL
MALAWI
ANGOLA MOZAMBIQUE
ZAMBIA
ZIMBABWE
MADAGASCAR
NAMIBIA
BOTSWANA
AUSTRALIA
ARGENTINA
SOUTH AFRICA

are working to stitch us all closer together."

LET'S BE FRIENDS!

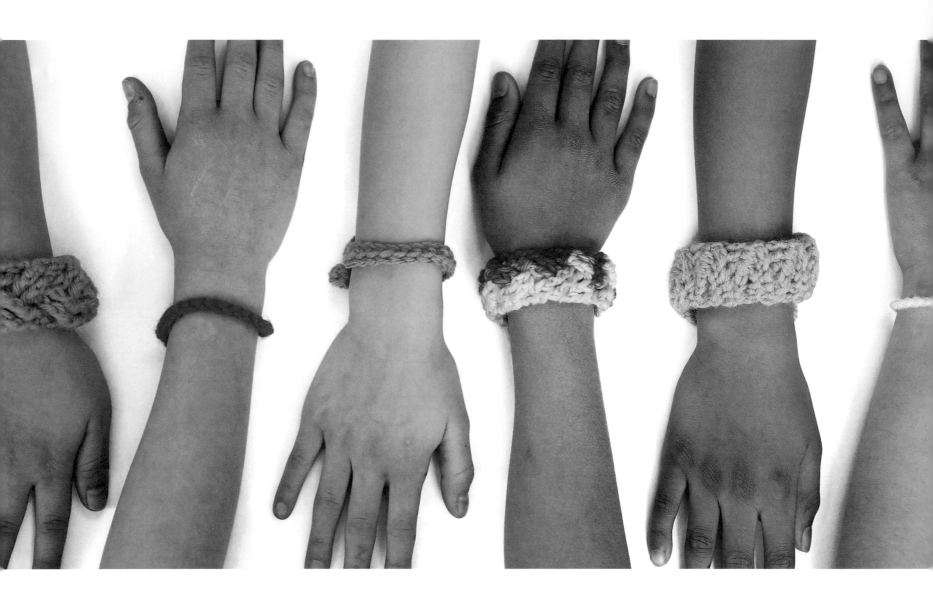

I love making friendship bracelets.

Here are three that you can try!

EASY CHAIN BRACELET
—*for beginning crocheters.*

All you have to do is make a foundation chain the size of your friend's wrist and fasten off!

SINGLE CROCHET BRACELET
—*for beginning crocheters.*

Make another foundation chain, but this time, work a single crochet into every stitch. Fasten off, and you've made a bracelet!

FANCY STITCH BRACELET
—*for beginning to advanced crocheters.*

As you continue to learn, you can design more complex bracelets using multiple stitches!

If you want to learn more about how to crochet, my advice is to do what I did—find tutorials online! You can even search for little things like *how to chain, how to fasten off,* and *how to make a single crochet.*

JONAH'S IDENTITY–
INSPIRED DISHCLOTH

I have designed a project that represents an important part of my story and my identity—a dishcloth, using the colors of the Ethiopian flag: green, yellow, and red. These colors remind me of the country where I was born, and they bring me joy. I hope that you can create a dishcloth that helps you tell part of your story and celebrates your identity. Most importantly, I hope that making it brings you joy.

Instructions
—for more advanced crocheters.

YARN: You can use any worsted cotton yarn (2.5 oz/120 yds/71g per ball) in 3 colors that represent you. Here I use Lily Sugar'n Cream.

A. Dark Pine
B. Yellow
C. Country Red

HOOK: Size H/5mm, or size needed to obtain gauge.

NOTIONS: Tapestry needle

GAUGE: 16 sc and ch-1 sps x 16 rows = 4 inches. Gauge is not critical for this project.

FINISHED MEASUREMENTS: Approximately 8 inches square (7 inches without border)

ABBREVIATIONS:

beg	=	*beginning*
ch(s)	=	*chain(s)*
g	=	*grams*
oz	=	*ounces*
rep	=	*repeat(s)*
sc	=	*single crochet(s)*
sk	=	*skip/skipped*
sl	=	*slip*
sp(s)	=	*space(s)*
st(s)	=	*stitch(es)*
WS	=	*wrong side*
yds	=	*yards*

PATTERN NOTES

- When joining colors, work to last 2 loops on hook of first color. Draw new color through last 2 loops and proceed.

- Last stitch is the chain-2 from the start of previous row. Work last single crochet of each row in the space created by the chain-2.

- When joining colors, leave a 6-inch tail to weave in at the end of the project.

DISHCLOTH PATTERN

ROW 1: With A, ch 28, sc in 4th ch from hook *(sk chs count as first sc and ch-1 sp)*, *ch 1, sk next ch, sc in next ch; rep from * to end of row, turn. *(14 sc, 13 ch-1 sps)*

ROW 2: Ch 2 *(counts as first sc and ch-1 sp)*, sc in first ch-1 sp, *ch 1, sk next sc, sc in next ch-1 sp; rep from * to last st *(see Pattern Notes)*, turn.

ROWS 3–10: Rep row 2. At end of row 10, change to B *(see Pattern Notes)*, fasten off A *(see Pattern Notes)*.

ROWS 11–19: Rep row 2. At end of row 19, change to C, fasten off B.

ROWS 20–28: Rep row 2, do not turn work. Fasten off unless adding optional border. Weave in ends if not working optional border.

BORDER (OPTIONAL)

Continuing with C, (ch 1, sc, ch 2, sc) in last st of last row *(corner)*, working down side in ends of rows, *sc in each row to next color, change to B and fasten off C; rep from * changing to A and fastening off B, (sc, ch 2, sc) in base of first st of row 1, sc in base of each st to last st of row 1, (sc, ch 2, sc) in last st, working along opposite side in ends of rows, sc in each row end changing colors as before to corner, (sc, ch 2, sc) in first st along top, sc in each st across, join with sl st in beg sc, fasten off. Weave in ends.

A SECRET LANGUAGE
FOR CROCHETERS!

CROCHET JARGON =
special acronyms, words, and expressions that are used by crocheters! Here are some of my favorites:

WIP (Work in Progress) **=**
My advice on WIPs—never have more than three at a time!

HOTH (Hot Off The Hook) **=**
Like many crocheters around the world, I love to share my projects on social media as soon as I finish them!

MGBTC (Must Get Back to Crocheting) **=**
My mom jokes that I don't need to use this acronym because... I am ALWAYS crocheting!

USO (Unstarted Object) **=**
You won't find any USOs at my house! As soon as I have the materials for a project, I dive in!

FROGGING/TO FROG =
ripping out your stitches and starting over at the point you made a mistake or starting completely over on a project.

Ribbit, ribbit sounds like rip it, rip it! I check my work often, and I am proud to say that I have never frogged an entire project.

YARN BARF =
the tangled mess of yarn that comes out of a skein if you pull out a strand from the center!

JONAH'S ADVICE

Be patient learning
—*it takes time!*

Have fun experimenting
—*you'll learn a lot this way!*

And remember…
HOOK
+ **YARN** to make
STITCHES =
(**BOOM!**) Another beautiful project complete!

So, that's me, so far at least. To all my friends around the world, thank you for your support and kindness. Remember to do what makes you happy and take some time to sit by a loved one and…

CROCHET AWAY!

PHOTO CREDITS

Cover:	Erin Harris
Front Jacket Flap:	Erin Harris
Front End Papers:	Jonah's Crochet Friends (Hands Collage);
	Erin Harris (Jonah's hands)
Page 3:	Erin Harris
Pages 4-21:	Larson Family Archive
Pages 22-23:	Erin Harris
Pages 24-25:	Erin Harris (all but cotton yarn);
	KWiL Publishing (cotton yarn)
Pages 26-27:	Erin Harris (Jonah's hands/Jonah);
	Jennifer Larson (Bobble stitch);
	KWiL Publishing (Waffle stitch, Moss stitch)
Pages 28-29:	Jonah's Crochet Friends
Pages 32-33:	Erin Harris
Pages 34-35:	Erin Harris
Pages 36:	Erin Harris
Pages 39:	Erin Harris
Pages 40:	Erin Harris
Back End Papers:	Erin Harris (Blankets);
	Jonah's Crochet Friends (Hands Collage)
Back Jacket Flap:	Erin Harris
Back:	Erin Harris

ACKNOWLEDGEMENTS

KWiL Publishing would like to extend our sincere thanks to the following people who made this book possible:

Karl Engebretson—BOOM!
Erin Harris
Daniel Kattman, Esq.
Mame Croze McCully

our beta readers and editors
(in particular S.N., J.N., T.K.W.—
J., M.D., B.H., W.H., L.P., M.B.,
& Mrs. Sentz's third-grade class)

Britt Schmiesing
Michael Sellick
Michelle Buckhanan
Christine Pingleton
Flavia Mildenberg
Amanda Zieba

Amy Lorentz with Gerrard-Hoeschler Realtors and ReFind Home

Jonah's incredible circle of crochet friends and, of course, the Larson Family

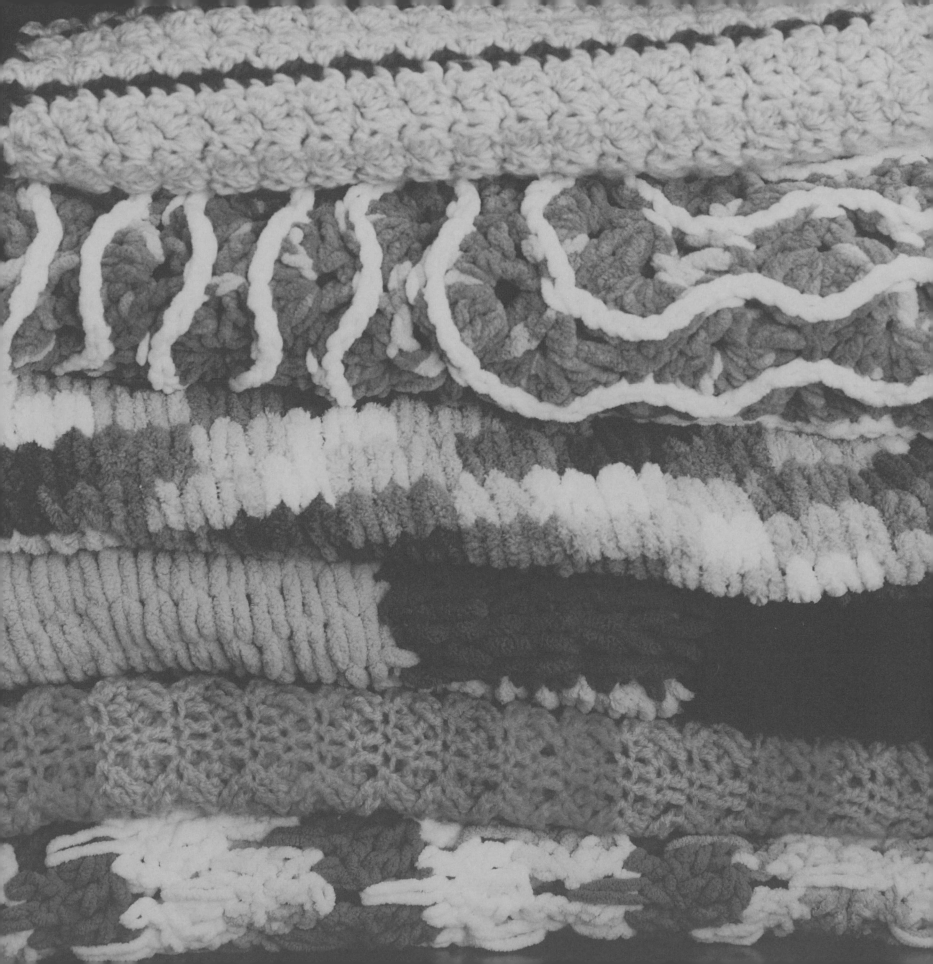